—— **Beginner's**
Guideline

Understanding the Business of Selling Digital Products

Creative Business Guideline

By Farhadur Rahim

START WITH
DEDICATION

To all the aspiring entrepreneurs and creators who dare to dream and strive to turn their ideas into profitable ventures. Your dedication, perseverance, and passion inspire us all. May this book serve as a guiding light on your journey from idea to income in the ever-evolving landscape of digital product sales. Here's to embracing challenges, seizing opportunities, and achieving success beyond your wildest dreams.

TABLE OF
CONTENTS

Introduction	00
What Is a Digital Product?	01
Examples of Digital Products	02
Marketing Your Own Products	11
Create Digital Products in 9 Steps	14
Launch a Product Successfully	20
Best Practices	26
Conclusion	33

INTRODUCTION

In today's digital age, opportunities for entrepreneurs to create and launch profitable digital products abound. From software applications to online courses, the possibilities are endless. However, amidst this sea of opportunity, navigating the complexities of digital product creation and launch can be daunting. That's where "From Idea to Income" comes in. This comprehensive guide is your roadmap to success in the digital marketplace.

With over 34 pages of invaluable insights, actionable strategies, and real-world examples, this book is designed to equip you with the knowledge and tools needed to thrive in the competitive world of digital product entrepreneurship.

Whether you're a seasoned industry professional or a newcomer to the scene, you'll find practical advice and expert guidance to help you every step of the way.

From conducting market research and generating killer product ideas to building and scaling your business, each chapter of "From Idea to Income" is packed with in-depth information and actionable tips to help you maximize your earning potential and achieve sustainable success.

So, if you're ready to turn your digital product dreams into reality and take your business to new heights, look no further. Let "From Idea to Income" be your ultimate guide on the journey to entrepreneurial success.

WHAT IS A DIGITAL PRODUCT?

The world of online commerce, digital products reign supreme. These are virtual goods that you can only access through electronic devices like laptops, smartphones, or tablets. Think of PDFs, eBooks, podcasts, and online courses as some popular examples.

One of the great things about digital products is their intangible nature. Because they don't exist in the physical realm, they're generally easier and more cost-effective to create, tweak, and distribute compared to traditional physical items.

The beauty of diving into the digital product business lies in its low barrier to entry. It's a realm where almost anyone can dip their toes and try their hand at entrepreneurship. But, as with any bustling marketplace, competition abounds. So, while the entry may be easy, standing out from the crowd requires creativity, innovation, and strategic thinking.

TOP-NOTCH EXAMPLES OF DIGITAL PRODUCTS

Let's take a closer look at the variety of digital products, illustrated with a handful of examples:

eBooks & Audiobooks

eBooks rank among the most sought-after information products that consumers are willing to invest in. What's even more promising is the projected growth of eBook readers, expected to soar up to 1.123 billion by the year 2027.

Adding to their appeal, eBooks are relatively easy to craft, requiring little more than written text and some basic graphics. Particularly in the realms of non-fiction and education, they prove to be lucrative ventures. You don't need to possess extraordinary creativity to dive into this field; simply draw from your expertise and passion to create valuable content. Whether it's crafting how-to guides, meal prep plans, workout routines, or detailed blueprints, the possibilities are endless.

Online Courses

Are you a natural educator? Do you excel in a specific field? If so, consider harnessing your talents and knowledge by creating online courses. They provide a fantastic opportunity to transform your expertise into a lucrative digital product.

After selecting your course topic, it's time to decide on your preferred delivery method — whether it's through audio, video, text, or any other format that suits your content best. Craft your curriculum with care, ensuring it aligns seamlessly with your chosen format, and then dive into content creation with enthusiasm and purpose.

In the past, developing and managing courses used to be a daunting and costly task, especially when it came to acquiring a Learning Management System (LMS). However, thanks to WordPress plugins, the process has become significantly more accessible and affordable. Now, you can effortlessly host your courses directly on your website, streamlining the entire educational experience for both you and your audience.

TOP-NOTCH EXAMPLES OF DIGITAL PRODUCTS

On the flip side, you have the option to utilize online course platforms like Udemy, Teachable, or Kajabi. These platforms offer a ready-made audience and streamline the process of monetizing your course without the need for extensive self-promotion.

Digital Art
For individuals skilled in graphic design, delving into the creation of digital art products presents an excellent avenue for generating income.

Below is a comprehensive yet not exhaustive compilation of digital products within this realm:

- Logos
- Brand kits
- Design templates
- Adobe files and templates
- Affinity Photo templates
- PowerPoint themes
- Banners
- Clip art
- Stock icons (vectors)
- Card designs

With the vast spectrum of artistic expressions available, digital art boasts a substantial customer base, catering to both corporate entities and individuals alike. Small business proprietors seek logos and flyers to enhance their branding efforts, while social media marketers crave visually captivating posts to engage their audience. Likewise, app developers rely on sleek UI designs to ensure an optimal user experience. In this digital age, the demand for digital art spans across various industries and sectors, making it a thriving field for artists and creatives to explore and thrive.

TOP-NOTCH EXAMPLES OF DIGITAL PRODUCTS

Video Content

When we think of VOD (Video on Demand) services like Netflix, we get a glimpse of the vast landscape of video content available today. However, the appeal of this dynamic format extends far beyond mere entertainment. It also encompasses a wide array of informational and educational subjects, making it a versatile tool for both learning and leisure.

Across the globe, adventurers are documenting their journeys via video blogs (vlogs) and finding lucrative opportunities. Meanwhile, a growing number are embracing innovative niches such as food vlogging, spotlighting their regional delicacies to captivated audiences.

There's an abundance of eager viewers ready to indulge in your travel documentaries, comedy sketches, gaming adventures, or captivating short films.

Templates

Templates serve as invaluable digital assets across various domains. They can serve as a wellspring of inspiration, guiding individuals to center their content effectively. Additionally, they offer a structured framework, enabling users to develop and refine their content with ease. Whether sparking creativity or streamlining the content creation process, templates are indispensable tools in the digital landscape.

Depending on your passions and skills, the variety of templates you can craft is endless. You might find joy in designing resumes that stand out, crafting compelling email templates, composing professional letters, jazzing up PowerPoint presentations, or even designing eye-catching business cards. Let your creativity flow and explore the endless possibilities of template creation.

With the ever-evolving landscape of design tools, there's a fresh category of templates that demands recognition: cloud-based design templates.

TOP-NOTCH EXAMPLES OF DIGITAL PRODUCTS

Online platforms such as Canva and VistaCreate provide a wealth of graphic templates, enabling users to effortlessly create stunning designs. For those with design expertise, these platforms also offer the opportunity to monetize their creations by selling them in a thriving marketplace.

Photography
The hunger for top-notch photographs remains constant, particularly within the realms of blogging, marketing, advertising, and website management.

A widely embraced avenue for leveraging your photography skills to generate income is by delving into the world of stock photography.

Here's how it works:

- You upload your imagery on the service platform,
- Consumers pay a fee to use your photo, and
- The fee splits between you and the platform.

In addition to the commonly known digital products like eBooks and online courses, there's a whole world of visual content waiting to be explored. Think drone photos, event snapshots, stylish backgrounds, and product imagery.

Jumping into photography as a digital product can feel like diving into a sea of competition. However, if you're able to consistently deliver top-notch images, price your services competitively, and hone in on the right audience, you'll find yourself riding the wave of success ahead of the pack.

Software
Projected at a robust annual growth rate of 6.5%, the software market is poised to soar to a staggering $812.9 billion in revenue by 2027. It's evident that venturing into software creation holds the promise of unparalleled profitability within the realm of digital products.

TOP-NOTCH EXAMPLES OF DIGITAL PRODUCTS

Software is an essential tool sought after by individuals, small business proprietors, and large corporations alike.

- WordPress plugins and themes
- Mobile apps
- Fitness apps
- Video games
- Windows/Android/iPhone apps
- Project management apps

While coding skills can certainly be advantageous when it comes to crafting software products, they're not always a prerequisite. Nonetheless, delving into software development can yield tremendous returns on investment.

ADVANTAGES OF MARKETING YOUR OWN DIGITAL PRODUCTS

Discover the myriad benefits of promoting your unique digital products. From unparalleled scalability and global accessibility to creative freedom and lucrative revenue streams, learn how marketing your own digital offerings can revolutionize your business journey.

Low-Cost
Creating a digital product not only saves you money but also minimizes risk. Let's explore the initial costs you can avoid by developing and introducing a digital product to the market.

- Raw materials
- Manufacturing
- Storing and warehousing
- Packing and fulfillment
- Shipping expenses

Furthermore, with digital products, there's no need for physical storefronts, eliminating expenses such as electricity bills, payroll, rent, POS software, and more.

In contrast to physical goods, selling digital products doesn't necessitate a large team to handle sales and management tasks. With the aid of software, numerous processes such as checkouts, demonstrations, delivery, and follow-up emails can be automated seamlessly, streamlining your operations and freeing up valuable time and resources.

Easier to Scale
In contrast to the logistical challenges faced by online stores selling physical products, the establishment of brick-and-mortar stores is often constrained by geographical limitations. However, the beauty of digital products lies in their limitless potential. They provide the opportunity to effortlessly penetrate various markets, broaden your audience base, and seamlessly access global markets with just a few clicks.

ADVANTAGES OF MARKETING YOUR OWN DIGITAL PRODUCTS

Consider this scenario: Let's say you're in the business of creating gaming avatars. One savvy approach is to engage directly with gaming enthusiasts through platforms like the Steam community, where you can showcase and sell your unique avatars. Moreover, if you notice a decline in demand within one region, you have the flexibility to pivot your attention to another region where the demand may be higher, ensuring your products remain relevant and in-demand.

Low Barriers to Entry
With the appropriate skill set and access to an electronic device such as a laptop, tablet, or smartphone, you possess the essential tools to dive into the market. Unlike traditional businesses reliant on various stakeholders like suppliers, manufacturers, and fulfillment vendors, your entry into the digital arena is self-reliant and independent.

However, the key determinant of your sustained success lies in your competitive edge. This is influenced by various factors such as pricing strategy, the value you provide, the caliber of your offerings, post-purchase support, and more.

High Profit Margins
By sidestepping hefty upfront expenses and operational overhead, you open the door to potentially lucrative profit margins. While you might still need to allocate funds for essentials like digital marketing, advertising, website hosting, and eCommerce platform subscriptions, the financial outlay tends to be significantly reduced in comparison.

Reduced production and operational expenses coupled with a broader reach among consumers open up opportunities to lower prices, slim down profit margins, and ultimately increase earnings through heightened sales volume.

Consider this scenario: Your paperback book might have to be priced at $50 to cover production costs and account for limited space in physical stores. However, its digital counterpart could be sold for just $5, potentially resulting in a tenfold increase in earnings.

ADVANTAGES OF MARKETING YOUR OWN DIGITAL PRODUCTS

Digital Products Last Forever
In the realm of digital goods, the possibilities are endless, and quality remains consistent over time. Unlike physical products, digital items don't degrade or suffer from wear and tear. Plus, you can bid farewell to storage woes and warehouse hassles, as everything exists in the virtual space.

Absolutely, digital products aren't immune to obsolescence. Yet, there's a silver lining: you can adapt to evolving needs and feedback without scrapping your entire product lineup. This might entail enhancing your offerings with fresh features, ironing out pesky bugs, or even tailoring experiences to individual users.
Transitioning forward, the beauty of digital products lies in their limitless availability. Unlike physical goods, there's no worry of running out of stock when it comes to digital products; you can sell infinite copies. Invest your efforts once, and reap the rewards of passive income for years to come.

HOW TO CREATE DIGITAL PRODUCTS IN 9 STEPS

In today's digital age, creating and launching digital products has become increasingly accessible and lucrative. Whether you're an entrepreneur, a freelancer, or a business owner, understanding the process of developing digital products is essential for success in various industries. From software applications to e-books, online courses, and digital artwork, the possibilities are endless. In this guide, we'll outline nine essential steps to help you navigate the journey of creating digital products effectively, from ideation to execution and beyond. Whether you're a novice or an experienced creator, these steps will provide you with valuable insights and strategies to bring your digital product ideas to life and maximize their potential in the marketplace.

1. Pick Your Niche
To start, selecting a niche that aligns with your interests, skills, and practicality is essential. Once you've identified a promising niche, consider the following:

- Is there a niche that I'm more interested in?
- What's the degree of my experience and skill set?
- How much competition exists in your niche?
- Do I have the prerequisites to pursue it?

As you navigate through your entrepreneurial journey, resist the urge to solely focus on a niche just because it appears to be more profitable. Remember, success isn't solely determined by the niche you choose; it's about your ability to address a genuine need or solve a problem effectively. With dedication and innovation, any niche has the potential to generate significant revenue. So, instead of fixating on perceived profitability, prioritize your passion and the value you can offer to your audience.

Certainly, while certain niches may indeed be saturated with competition, your passion and dedication will serve as powerful catalysts in overcoming any challenges posed by rivals.

HOW TO CREATE DIGITAL PRODUCTS IN 9 STEPS

2. Conduct Market Research
Once you've pinpointed your niche, it's time to delve into market research to zero in on your ideal audience, understand their challenges, and assess your potential competitors.

At this point, your primary objective should be to discover: **What solution can I offer that individuals are willing to pay me for?**

Here are some of the ways you could conduct your market research:

- Explore social media to see what's trending.
- Join niche-specific groups on LinkedIn and other social networks to find out topics of discussion.
- Use Google Trends and Google Keyword Planner to know what people are searching for.

Now, onto the exciting stage of narrowing down your product ideas! It's essential to focus on identifying concepts that meet two critical criteria: high demand and low competition. Take the time to brainstorm and explore various possibilities. Once you have a list, delve into market research to understand what products are already available and where the gaps lie. Your goal is to uncover opportunities to offer something unique and valuable, setting yourself apart from the competition.

3. Understand Your Target Audience
Having a precise grasp of your target audience's pain points is pivotal for product development. To gain a comprehensive insight into your prospective customers, crafting a buyer persona is essential. This persona should encompass key elements such as:

- Personal demographics: age, gender, location, income level;
- Professional demographics (business-specific details);
- Goals, challenges, priorities, motivations, and values;
- Shopping preferences.

HOW TO CREATE DIGITAL PRODUCTS IN 9 STEPS

Another effective approach is to send tailored surveys aimed at delving into your audience's challenges and expectations. Here are some sample questions to consider:

- What's your biggest struggle when it comes to [insert your niche]?
- Would you purchase a product that could solve this problem?
- If I could help you with one thing, what would it be?
- If I make a guide on [insert topic], what format would I like? (List formats like video, print, and audio).
- How much would you be willing to spend on a product that could [insert your solution]?

4. Write a Positioning Statement

At this stage, you've likely brainstormed several ideas for your upcoming digital product. Now, it's crucial to craft a positioning statement to gain a clear understanding of your product's essence. This strategic step will not only enhance your product's clarity but also pave the way for future collaborations with influencers and industry leaders.

Crafting your positioning statement necessitates addressing the following inquiries:

- Who is your product for?
- What is your product niche?
- What does your product do?
- What are your product's benefits?
- What separates your product from what's already being offered?

5. Set Competitive Pricing

As you embark on your entrepreneurial journey, it's wise to initially price your digital products slightly lower than your top competitors. For instance, if you've identified seven competitors and the lowest-priced product among them is $10, consider setting your price at $8 or $9.

HOW TO CREATE DIGITAL PRODUCTS IN 9 STEPS

This strategy helps you attract customers while establishing your presence in the market. As you gain traction and recognition, you can gradually adjust your pricing strategy accordingly. Some other pricing strategies which you can consider:

- Use tiered pricing, especially for membership/subscription
- Demonstrate how much they're saving with packages
- Offer a free plan or a free trial
- Include price comparison to assert the market's best price

6. Set Up a Waiting List
Don't let all your hard work go to waste by launching a digital product that falls flat! Building a waiting list can be a game-changer in validating your product idea and boosting its chances of success.

The key is to drum up excitement and build anticipation around your product. The more people show interest by signing up on your waiting list, the more confident you can feel about your product's potential.

Consider creating a dedicated landing page for your product idea. Utilize SEO strategies to ensure the page gets noticed by search engines, and provide informative content to educate your target audience about your product's features and benefits.

Offering something of value for free—like a sneak peek of your course, a downloadable resource, or exclusive access to a webinar—in exchange for email sign-ups is a smart move. This not only grows your email list but also keeps potential customers engaged and interested.

Once you've built your email list, leverage it with targeted email marketing campaigns to nurture your leads and keep the excitement alive. With the right strategy, you'll be well on your way to a successful product launch.

HOW TO CREATE DIGITAL PRODUCTS IN 9 STEPS

7. Post Free Content
Now, let's explore a more indirect approach to lead people to your landing page — leveraging free content.

Crafting top-notch content on your social media platforms and website is a fantastic strategy for this phase. Ensure your content remains pertinent to your audience, stays current, captivates attention, and offers real value.

Successfully executing this step can result in a growing and loyal following. Moreover, influential figures in your industry, notable brands, and key influencers might even share your content, amplifying your visibility.

Guest posting emerges as another potent tool to drive traffic to your product page and expand your waiting list.

Here's the gist: Identify influential blogs within your niche and propose topics you can contribute to. Once accepted, you'll provide guest articles, leveraging their established audience to your advantage.

Seize this opportunity to enlighten your target audience about your digital product, guiding them back to your channels via embedded links.

8. Create Minimum Viable Product
Prior to launching your final product, consider developing an MVP or beta version to assess its viability, gather feedback, and implement essential improvements.

For beta testing, assemble a select group of testers comprising potential buyers and industry influencers. Provide them with complimentary access to the beta version and solicit their feedback through surveys to gauge their user experience and gather valuable insights for refinement.

This could help you find out:

- If your product is solving the "X" problem successfully.

HOW TO CREATE DIGITAL PRODUCTS IN 9 STEPS

- If your product offers the best value for money.
- What problems were encountered while running your product?
- What was felt missing in your product?
- Improvement suggestions for your product.

Harness the gathered data to refine your digital product prior to its official launch. Additionally, consider soliciting testimonials from satisfied users to showcase positive experiences. Share these testimonials on your product page to establish credibility and foster trust with your audience.

9. Select Tools and Platform

Once your masterpiece is polished and ready for the world, the next step is finding the perfect platform to showcase and sell it. This is where your decision-making prowess comes into play.

- Where will you sell your digital product?
- How will you collect payment?
- How will you collect and store customer data?

Consider harnessing the power of WordPress as your go-to content management system for this endeavor. Its robust capabilities make it a reliable choice for building your online platform.

Within WordPress, you'll find an extensive library of themes and plugins that can be tailored to suit your specific eCommerce needs. From facilitating on-site payment processing to implementing subscription billing, email marketing tools, social sharing buttons, and even software licensing features, the possibilities are endless.

Embrace the versatility of WordPress to craft a fully customized eCommerce website equipped with all the essential functionalities required for success in the digital marketplace.

HOW TO LAUNCH A PRODUCT SUCCESSFULLY

With your digital product primed and polished, it's time to ensure a successful launch. Here's your roadmap to a triumphant debut:

Choose an Appropriate Launch Time
Similar to physical goods, digital products can also be influenced by seasonality. For instance, there might be an uptick in spending during the winter months as individuals prefer to cozy up indoors.

Your niche may have its trending wave based on seasonal dynamics:

- Thinking about releasing your health and wellness eBook? Aim for a January launch to align with the surge of New Year's resolutions.

- Crafted a concise course to boost exam performance? Consider launching it a month or two prior to exam dates for maximum impact.

- Created a DIY wedding planner? Launch it during the winter months to assist couples in planning their spring or summer weddings.

Execute Early Marketing Strategy
Now is the time to start the full-fledged promotion of your launch and get people excited about it. Here are some ways you could do that:

- Intrigue your audience with a captivating "Coming Soon" page featuring an enticing countdown timer, igniting anticipation and curiosity about your upcoming digital offering.

- Provide sneak peeks and engaging demos to acquaint your audience with the unique features and benefits of your digital product, building excitement and familiarity before its official launch.

HOW TO LAUNCH A PRODUCT SUCCESSFULLY

- Maintain a consistent presence on your social media platforms by scheduling regular posts, fostering ongoing interest and engagement among your audience, and keeping them eagerly awaiting the release of your digital masterpiece.

Set Promotional Pricing
Embracing promotional pricing strategies can be a powerful tool to reduce barriers and enhance the accessibility of your product. By implementing these tactics, you can effectively minimize friction and encourage more customers to engage with your offering. Here are some innovative promotional pricing strategies to consider integrating into your product's marketing approach:

- Limited-Time Offers: Create a sense of urgency by offering special discounts or deals for a limited period. This strategy prompts customers to make quicker purchasing decisions to take advantage of the temporary savings, driving immediate sales.

- Bundle Discounts: Bundle complementary products or services together and offer them at a discounted rate compared to purchasing each item individually. This strategy not only incentivizes customers to buy more but also enhances the overall value proposition of your offerings.

- First-Time Customer Discounts: Offer exclusive discounts or promotions to first-time customers as an incentive to try out your product. This approach can help attract new customers and encourage them to experience the value your product provides at a reduced cost.

- Tiered Pricing: Implement tiered pricing structures that cater to different customer segments based on their needs and budget. By offering multiple pricing options, you provide flexibility and cater to a broader range of customers, minimizing friction and increasing conversion rates.

HOW TO LAUNCH A PRODUCT SUCCESSFULLY

- Referral Programs: Encourage existing customers to refer friends, family, or colleagues to your product by offering rewards or discounts for successful referrals. This strategy not only incentivizes word-of-mouth marketing but also fosters customer loyalty and engagement.

- ·Seasonal Promotions: Capitalize on seasonal trends, holidays, or special events by offering promotions or discounts aligned with the occasion. Seasonal promotions can create excitement and urgency, driving sales and boosting brand visibility during key periods.

- Abandoned Cart Discounts: Implement automated email sequences to follow up with customers who abandon their carts without completing the purchase. Offer special discounts or incentives to entice them to return and complete their transaction, reducing cart abandonment rates.

- Flash Sales: Organize spontaneous flash sales with limited inventory or time frames to generate excitement and urgency among your audience. Flash sales can create a buzz around your product and drive immediate sales while also clearing excess inventory.

By incorporating these promotional pricing strategies into your marketing arsenal, you can effectively minimize friction in your product's path and accelerate its adoption and success in the market.

Extend Your Digital Marketing Channels
At this point, you've likely utilized various promotional tactics such as blogging, guest posting, email marketing, and social media to market your digital product. Now, it's time to elevate your strategy by enlisting strategic launch partners who can serve as authentic advocates for your product.

Imagine the impact of having a trusted YouTuber or influencer share their positive experience with your product. This can significantly boost trust in your brand among their followers. Just think about the potential outreach when partnering with an influencer boasting millions of followers on platforms like Facebook!

HOW TO LAUNCH A PRODUCT SUCCESSFULLY

Consider collaborating with these partners for paid promotions, either through a fixed payment or an affiliate arrangement. With the latter, the promoter earns a percentage of each sale made through their unique affiliate link. This approach can incentivize partners to actively promote your product, driving sales and expanding your reach even further.

Execute Final Quality Assurance
Prior to releasing the ultimate iteration of your product, it is crucial to subject it to thorough testing to ensure quality assurance.

- Does your product work seamlessly?
- Can it handle heavy site loads and scaling?
- Does your product meet the market's expectations?
- How well have you incorporated the feedback that was initially gathered?

Evaluate your digital products using these metrics and implement necessary modifications to ensure perfection.

Monitor Your Business
After the release of your digital product, it's crucial to conduct an analysis of key performance indicators (KPIs) to evaluate its success and identify areas for enhancement. These KPIs provide valuable insights into various aspects of your product's performance. Examples of KPIs include:

- Paid vs. organic traffic
- Bounce and churn rates
- Number of sessions and session durations
- Customer lifetime value

In addition to assessing your website, consider implementing marketing tactics and lead generation strategies.

HOW TO LAUNCH A PRODUCT SUCCESSFULLY

Ask For Feedback

Gathering feedback directly from your customers is a crucial method to assess their response to your digital product and utilize it for enhancements. There are numerous avenues through which you can gather feedback:

Automated Email Campaigns

Utilizing your email marketing platform, you have the capability to automate the process of collecting feedback through emails.

To enable this feature, ensure that your system is configured to automatically add new customers to your email subscriber list. Subsequently, set up scheduled emails to be dispatched a few weeks post-purchase, prompting customers to share their experiences with your product. This timeframe allows ample opportunity for customers to thoroughly evaluate your offering.

Utilizing Customer Surveys

An efficient method for collecting feedback swiftly is by implementing a customer survey form. This approach is particularly beneficial for brands that have identified crucial inquiries, and where open-ended responses may not be as insightful.

It's advantageous to formulate questions regarding the solution you intend to offer and delve into specific aspects of the user experience.

Encourage Feedback on Your Website

Enhance interaction on your website by integrating a feedback mechanism. Consider incorporating a designated text input field on your site labeled, "We'd love to hear from you about [product name]". Alternatively, provide a survey link to gather more specific insights and opinions.

Take it From There

Introducing a digital product marks the commencement of a cyclical journey. Moving forward, you'll employ familiar strategies to expand your business's reach.

HOW TO LAUNCH A PRODUCT SUCCESSFULLY

Consider, for instance, the utilization of email sequencing. It can be harnessed not only for acquiring leads but also for nurturing existing customers, fostering loyalty, and maximizing retention rates.

- Cultivate sequences: Disseminate informative content to acquaint potential customers with your brand and products. Illuminate the issues your product addresses and demonstrate how they can harness its benefits.

- Orientation sequences: Upon sign-up, guide users through the utilization of your digital offering. Expand this process to demonstrate potential integrations with their existing business operations.

- Transition sequences: During the final stage, provide targeted sales-oriented content. Showcase case studies, esteemed clientele, success narratives, and endorsements to encourage conversion.

In addition to utilizing email campaigns, maintaining a consistent guest-posting strategy remains crucial for attracting fresh prospects. Expanding your network of affiliates can further bolster sales, while continuing to generate informative blog posts can enhance your brand's credibility and attract organic traffic.

Moreover, it's advisable to optimize conversion rates by investing in paid advertising across various platforms such as LinkedIn, Facebook, Instagram, and Google Ads. This diversified approach ensures wider reach and increased visibility, ultimately driving growth and success for your business.

BEST PRACTICES

FOR CREATING DIGITAL PRODUCTS

In today's rapidly evolving digital landscape, creating successful digital products requires a combination of innovation, user-centric design, and adherence to best practices. Whether developing mobile apps, websites, or software solutions, the process demands careful planning, execution, and iteration to meet the ever-changing needs and expectations of users. This introduction delves into key principles and strategies encompassing best practices for creating digital products, emphasizing the importance of user experience, scalability, and continuous improvement in driving product success.

BEST PRACTICES

FOR CREATING DIGITAL PRODUCTS

1. Stick to User-Centered Approach
Employing a user-centric strategy entails placing your users squarely at the heart of your product journey. This approach necessitates a thorough comprehension and acknowledgment of their requirements, drives, challenges, and actions when making decisions.

By adopting a user-centric methodology, meticulous attention is paid to user intricacies. This enables the incorporation of features that enhance user experience while redirecting attention to areas of genuine significance.

The outcome? Enhanced customer satisfaction and unwavering loyalty.

BEST PRACTICES

FOR CREATING DIGITAL PRODUCTS

2. Develop Roadmap and Set Clear Goals
Crafting a comprehensive product roadmap is pivotal for delineating your goals, objectives, and the timeline for your product launch. Firstly, it ensures alignment among all members of the product development team, fostering cohesive efforts towards a shared vision. Moreover, it serves as a guiding framework, indicating opportune moments for decision-making to steer the product in the desired direction. This roadmap also serves as a reference point for pre-launch activities, offering clarity and coherence in your ventures.

By establishing clear objectives, you can effectively channel your team's energy and resources towards their attainment. This process aids in prioritizing tasks, enhancing efficiency, and ultimately reducing the time required for the product launch.

BEST PRACTICES

FOR CREATING DIGITAL PRODUCTS

3. Create a Culture of Experimentation
Engaging in experiments provides the opportunity to continually test fresh product concepts and functionalities.

Embracing this approach not only fosters the development of innovative solutions but also safeguards against investing in initiatives that may ultimately falter.

As you explore fresh experiments, leverage data analytics to guide your decision-making process.

As an illustration, an elevated churn rate might stem from the elevated difficulty level of your assessments. Should you observe subpar performances in the tests, adjusting the difficulty level downwards could be a potential strategy to assess whether it enhances customer retention.

BEST PRACTICES

FOR CREATING DIGITAL PRODUCTS

4. Provide a Personalized Experience
Enhancing user experience significantly can be achieved through offering personalized interactions. This aspect focuses on tailoring the user's journey to make them feel uniquely addressed by the product.

Providing exceptional service to your clientele involves leveraging their data insights to deliver tailored notifications, suggestions, individualized trends, and statistical analyses.

Furthermore, you have the opportunity to surpass user expectations by providing incentives for their loyalty to your brand. This might entail:

- Emails of gratitude for X years of loyalty.
- Award for purchasing from you after a long time.
- Posters to celebrate the user's event (top customer of the month, user's birthday, etc.)

BEST PRACTICES

FOR CREATING DIGITAL PRODUCTS

5. Offer a Visual Treat
The presentation of your digital product and its portrayal to your audience holds significant sway. For example, imbuing your electronic card with vibrant design elements, playful illustrations, or unconventional fonts can transform it into a remarkably lifelike creation.

Here's how to create visually appealing work:

- Ensure that the color palette aligns with your brand's identity and personality.
- Incorporate 3D animations wherever feasible to enhance engagement.
- Maintain consistency in font style and size throughout the digital product.
- Strategically position essential buttons like signup and buy now in easily accessible areas.
- Ensure that all content is appropriately sized to fit within the screen dimensions.

BEST PRACTICES

FOR CREATING DIGITAL PRODUCTS

6. Keep Learning
Remaining cognizant of market dynamics and emerging industry trends is crucial for maintaining a competitive edge. By staying informed about industry developments, you can anticipate evolving customer preferences and adjust your product accordingly.

This awareness also enables you to assess your product's positioning in the market and identify necessary adaptations. Additionally, it's essential to stay abreast of new technologies and tools that can enhance your digital product and elevate the customer experience.

Gaining industry-specific insights through various channels such as reading survey reports, attending conferences, pursuing relevant courses, and networking with key stakeholders is invaluable. Continuous learning empowers you to make well-informed decisions and secure the competitive advantage necessary to sustain the success of your digital business.

CONCLUSION

Let's summarize the process of conceptualizing and launching a digital product in a concise manner:

01 Perform thorough market research and construct a detailed buyer persona to understand your target audience's needs and preferences.

02 Craft a minimum viable product (MVP) to swiftly validate your concept and gauge market demand effectively.

03 Foster a supportive community around your digital product to engage users, gather insights, and cultivate loyalty.

04 Validate your digital product idea through various channels, including surveys, interviews, and prototype testing, to ensure alignment with user expectations.

05 Conduct comprehensive testing of your MVP to identify areas for improvement and refine its functionality, usability, and overall user experience.

06 Implement pre-launch and post-launch promotional strategies to generate anticipation, attract users, and sustain momentum for your digital product.

07 Thoroughly assess the functionality and performance of your digital product to confirm that all features operate seamlessly and meet user requirements.

08 Continuously gather user feedback through analytics, surveys, and user testing to identify opportunities for enhancement and iteration, ensuring ongoing refinement and optimization.

This extensive manual for launching a digital product can provide valuable guidance for navigating the process effectively. Despite its perceived complexity, creating a digital product is often simpler compared to developing a physical one. One of its most advantageous aspects is the potential for higher profit margins, coupled with the ease of scalability.